Cre

CURSIVE & SPELLING

Do-It-Yourself

JOURNAL

READ, WRITE, SPELL & DRAW

A Poetry & Cursive Coloring Book

SARAH JANISSE BROWN

The Thinking Tree Publishing Company LLC 2016 - Poems & Cover Art by Sarah J. Brown
Copyright 2016 Do Not Copy - DyslexiaGames.com—Dyslexie Font

FunSchoolingBooks.com

INSTRUCTIONS
FOR PARENTS OR TEACHERS:

1. If the child can not read well, read each poem four times, pointing to each word as you read it. Many of the words are sight words that do not follow the rules of phonics. The child must be able to recognize each word visually.

2. Ask the child to repeat after you for the 3rd and 4th readings, the goal is for the child to memorize the rhyme.

3. Provide the child with colorful gel pens and one black gel pen.

4. Help the child to understand the instructions on each page. Sometimes the child will color the words in the poem, write the full poem, color a picture, create a comic, design a character, or draw the missing parts.

175 PRACTICAL SPELLING WORDS

almost	dog	happy
animals	dolphin	hide
apples	doors	hiking
art	down	home
baby	dream	hours
bakes	eagle	house
beach	earth	hunt
because	eat	ice-cream
best	eating	inside
birds	every	jump
boat	explored	just
book	face	kid
boot	favorite	king
born	fires	know
cake	fit	late
cakes	float	learn
camping	fluffy	light
canary	fly	listen
canoe	food	little
castle	found	live
cat	friend	looked
chew	friends	looking
chicken	frogs	lost
cook	from	love
could	going	loves
create	greatest	makes
cupcakes	grow	many
cute	had	mars
dance	hallway	mind

175 PRACTICAL SPELLING WORDS

mood	royal	swim
moon	run	tall
much	running	tasted
music	Saturday	teeth
my	sea	them
named	search	they
night	searched	things
outside	seashells	think
owl	seek	tiny
pancake	shaggy	treats
pencil	shall	tree
perfect	shelf	true
pies	shines	use
pig	simple	wake
pillows	sing	want
planet	sister	was
planted	size	watch
play	small	what
powers	smell	where
prance	smile	while
princess	snacks	white
puppy	something	windows
reached	song	woods
remember	stacked	world
return	start	would
rocket	stay	year
roof	stories	yesterday
rooster	summer	yummy
row	sweets	

175 PRACTICAL SPELLING IN CURSIVE

almost	cake	dance
animals	cakes	dog
apples	camping	dolphin
art	canary	doors
baby	canoe	down
bakes	castle	dream
beach	cat	eagle
because	chew	earth
best	chicken	eat
birds	cook	eating
boat	could	every
book	create	explored
boot	cupcakes	face
born	cute	favorite

fires	hallway	late
fit	happy	learn
float	hide	light
fluffy	hiking	listen
fly	home	little
food	hours	live
found	house	looked
friend	hunt	looking
friends	ice-cream	lost
frogs	inside	love
from	jump	loves
going	just	makes
greatest	kid	many
grow	king	mars
had	know	mind

175 SPELLING WORDS IN CURSIVE

mood
moon
much
music
my
named
night
outside
owl
pancake
pencil
perfect
pies
pig
pillows

planet
planted
play
powers
prance
princess
puppy
reached
remember
return
rocket
roof
rooster
row
royal

running
Saturday
sea
search
searched
seashells
seek
shaggy
shall
shelf
shines
simple
sing
sister
size

small	them	white
smell	they	windows
smile	things	woods
snacks	think	world
something	tiny	would
song	treats	year
stacked	tree	yesterday
start	true	yummy
stay	use	
stories	wake	
summer	want	
sweets	was	
swim	watch	
tall	what	
tasted	where	
teeth	while	

CREATIVE COMICS
DESIGN YOUR OWN CHARACTERS HERE

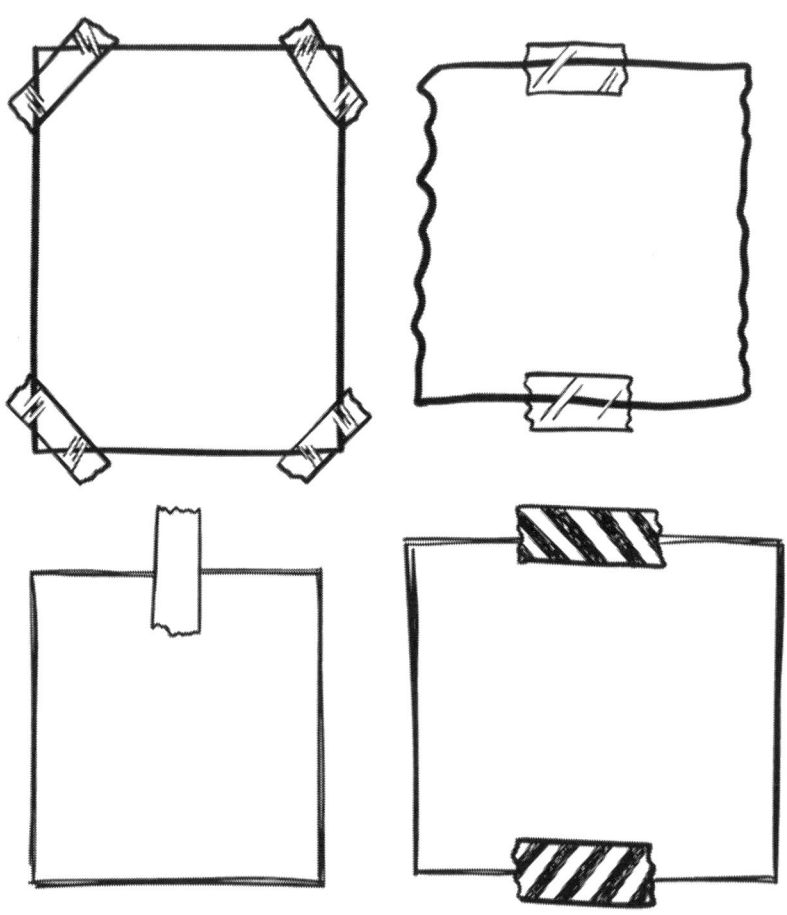

Study these Characters for Inspiration

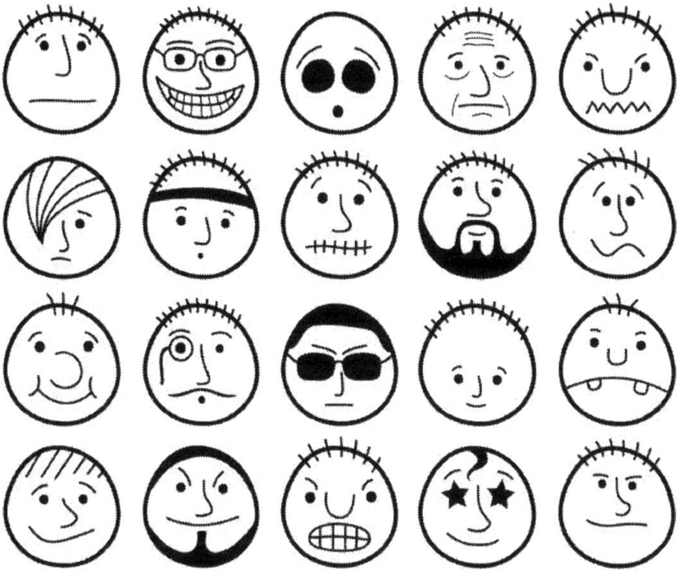

Use Your own Characters in this Comic Strip

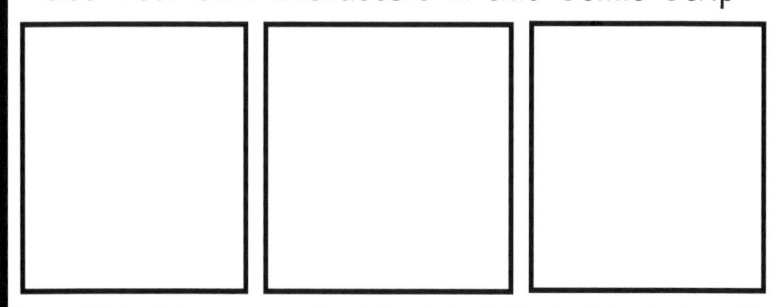

MUSIC TIME

Turn up the music

play my favorite song.

I will listen to music

all day long.

My cats will dance.

My dogs will sing.

My horse will prance.

And we will clean.

COLOR ME!

MUSIC TIME

TURN UP THE MUSIC
PLAY MY FAVORITE SONG.
I WILL LISTEN TO MUSIC
ALL DAY LONG.
MY CATS WILL DANCE.
MY DOGS WILL SING.
MY HORSE WILL PRANCE.
AND WE WILL CLEAN.

Use seven different colors to color all the words in this poem.

DRAW THE MISSING PARTS:

CREATE A COMIC
WITH THESE SPELLING WORDS:

music

play

favorite

song

listen

dance

sing

prance

MUSIC TIME

Turn up the music
play my favorite song.
I will listen to music
all day long.
My cats will dance.
My dogs will sing.
My horse will prance.
and we will clean.

COPY THE POEM HERE:

SPELLING TIME

Choose a letter:

Look in this book for 5 words that contain this letter.

1._____
2._____
3._____
4._____
5._____

WRITE THESE FIVE WORDS IN CURSIVE

almost	baby	best
animals	bakes	birds
apples	beach	boat
art	because	book

TRY WRITING YOUR SPELLING WORDS WITH A COMIC STYLE FONT!

OUTER SPACE

Take a rocket
To the moon.
Fly to mars,
but come home soon.
return to earth,
Your home and mine.
The only planet
of its kind.

COLOR ME!

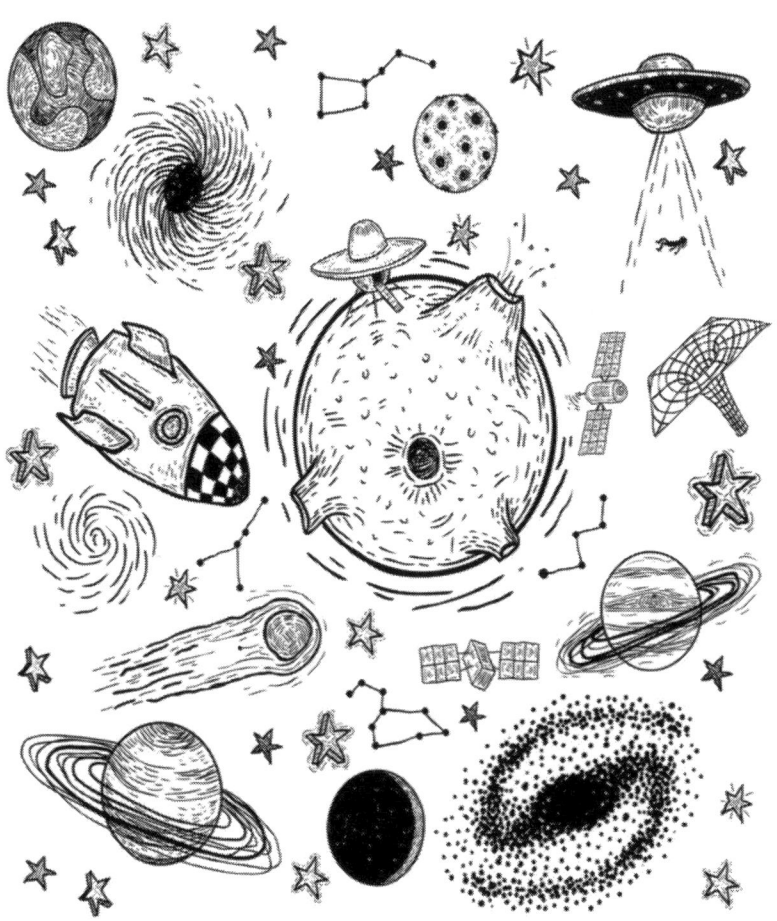

CREATIVE COMICS
DESIGN YOUR OWN CHARACTERS HERE

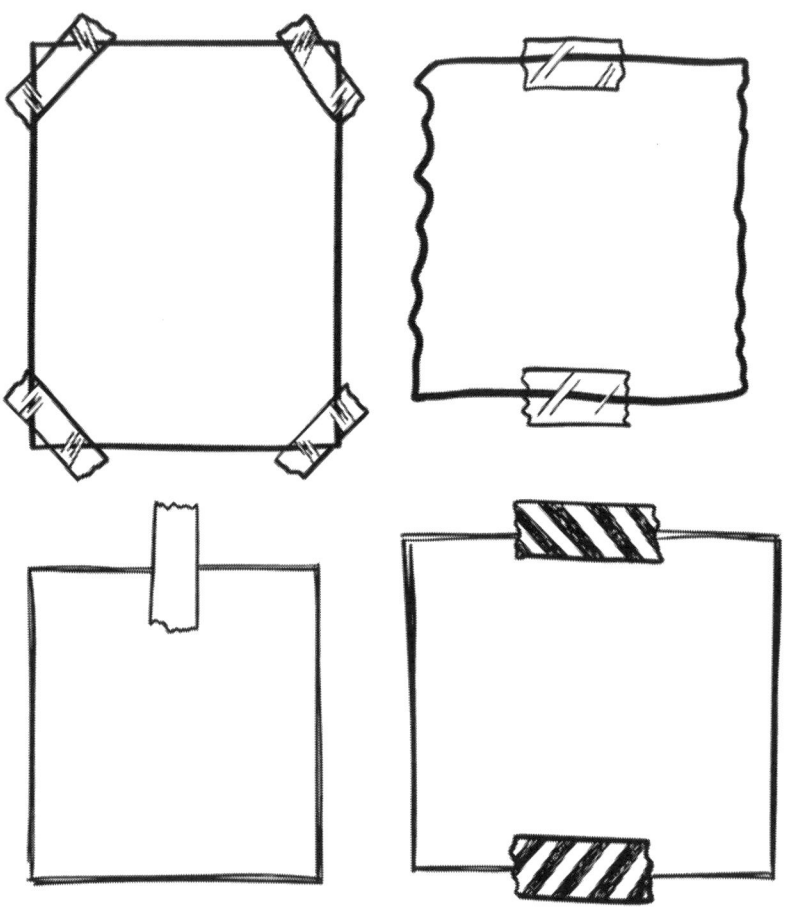

Study these Characters for Inspiration

Use Your own Characters in this Comic Strip

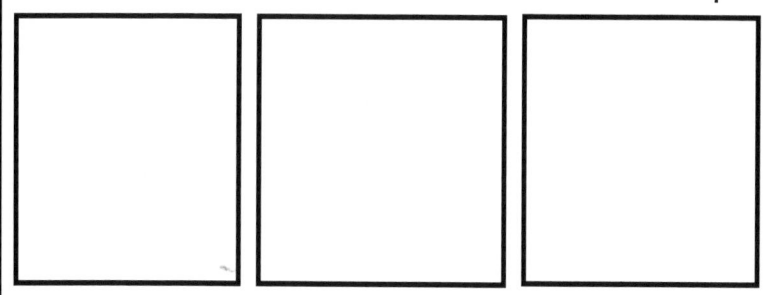

OUTER SPACE

Take a _____
to the _____.
Fly to _____,
but come home _____.
Return to _____,
your home and _____.
The only _____
of its _____.

DRAW THE MISSING PARTS:

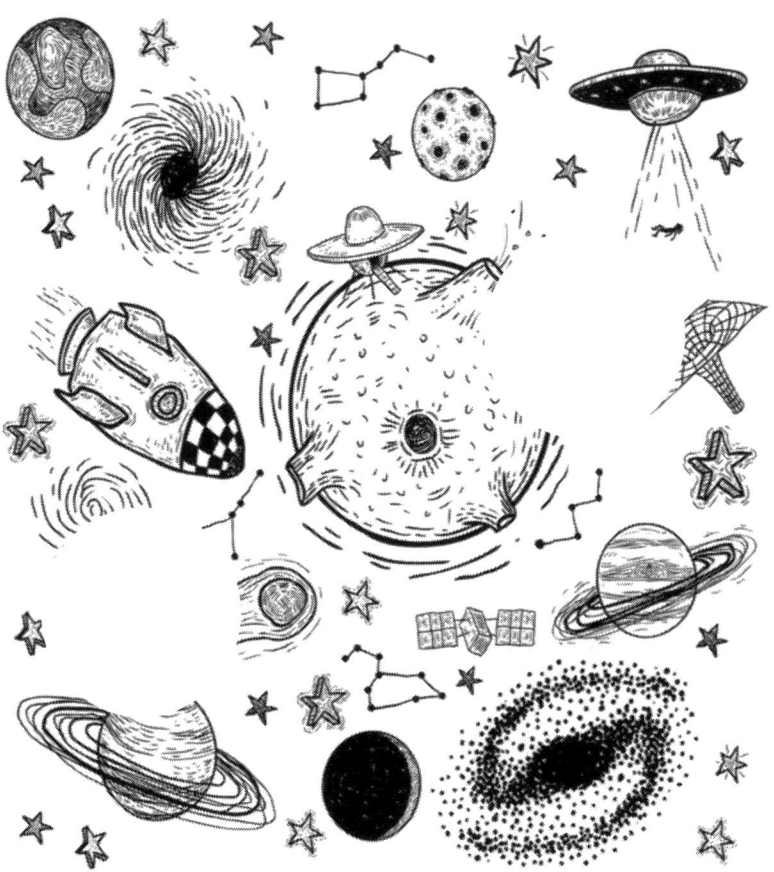

CREATE A COMIC
WITH THESE SPELLING WORDS:

 rocket

moon

 fly

mars

 return

earth

 planet

 home

SPELLING TIME

Choose a letter:

Look in this book for 5 words that contain this letter.

1._____
2._____
3._____
4._____
5._____

WRITE THESE FIVE WORDS IN CURSIVE

OUTER SPACE

Take a rocket
to the moon.
Fly to mars
but come home soon.
Return to earth,
your home and mine.
The only planet
of its kind.

COPY THE POEM HERE:

CREATIVE COMICS
DESIGN YOUR OWN CHARACTERS HERE

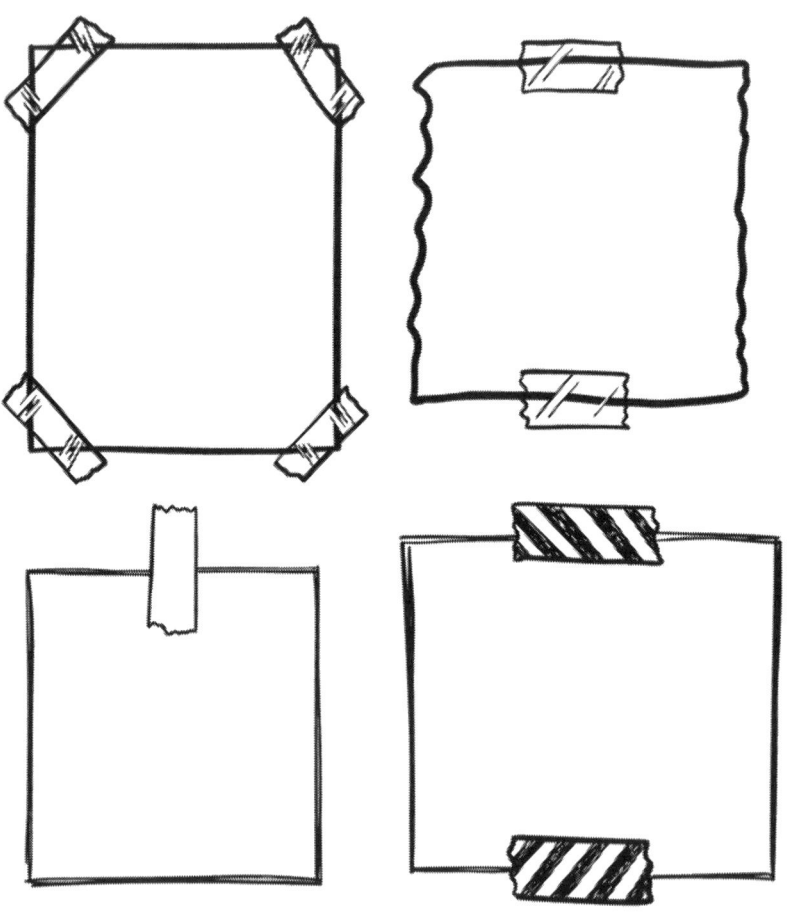

Study these Characters for Inspiration

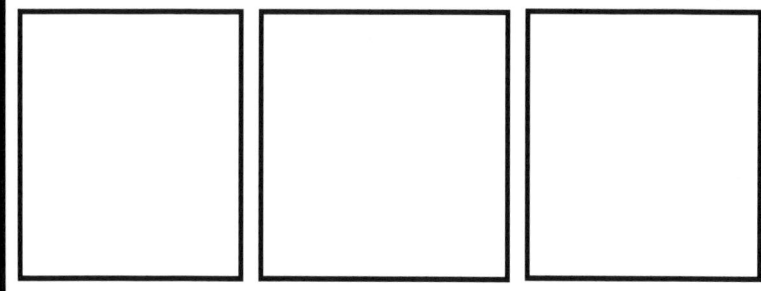

Use Your own Characters in this Comic Strip

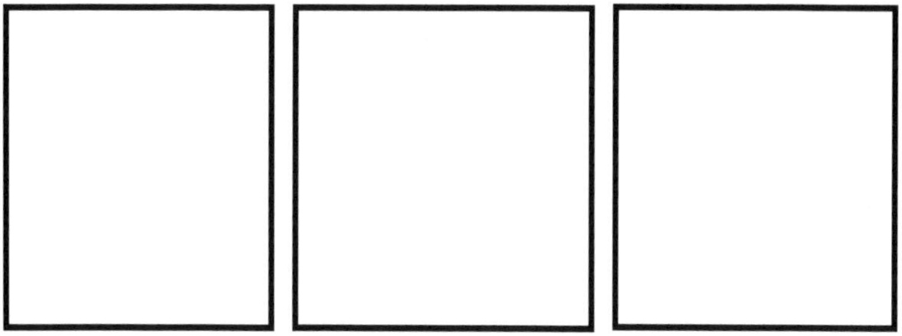

THE BOOK SHELF

I am looking
for a book,
I want to learn
new things.
So many books
are on my shelf,
To help me
learn new things.

COLOR ME!

THE BOOK SHELF

I AM LOOKING
FOR A BOOK,
I WANT TO LEARN
NEW THINGS.
SO MANY BOOKS
ARE ON MY SHELF,
TO HELP ME
LEARN NEW THINGS.

Use five different colors to color all the words in this poem.

DRAW THE MISSING PARTS:

CREATE A COMIC
WITH THESE SPELLING WORDS:

looking

book

want

things

learn

many

shelf

THE BOOK SHELF

I am looking
for a book,
I want to learn
new things.
So many books
are on my shelf,
To help me
learn new things.

COPY THE POEM HERE:

cake	castle	could
camping	cat	create
canary	chew	cupcakes
canoe	chicken	cute
cakes	cook	

TRY WRITING YOUR SPELLING WORDS WITH A COMIC STYLE FONT!

CREATIVE COMICS
DESIGN YOUR OWN CHARACTERS HERE

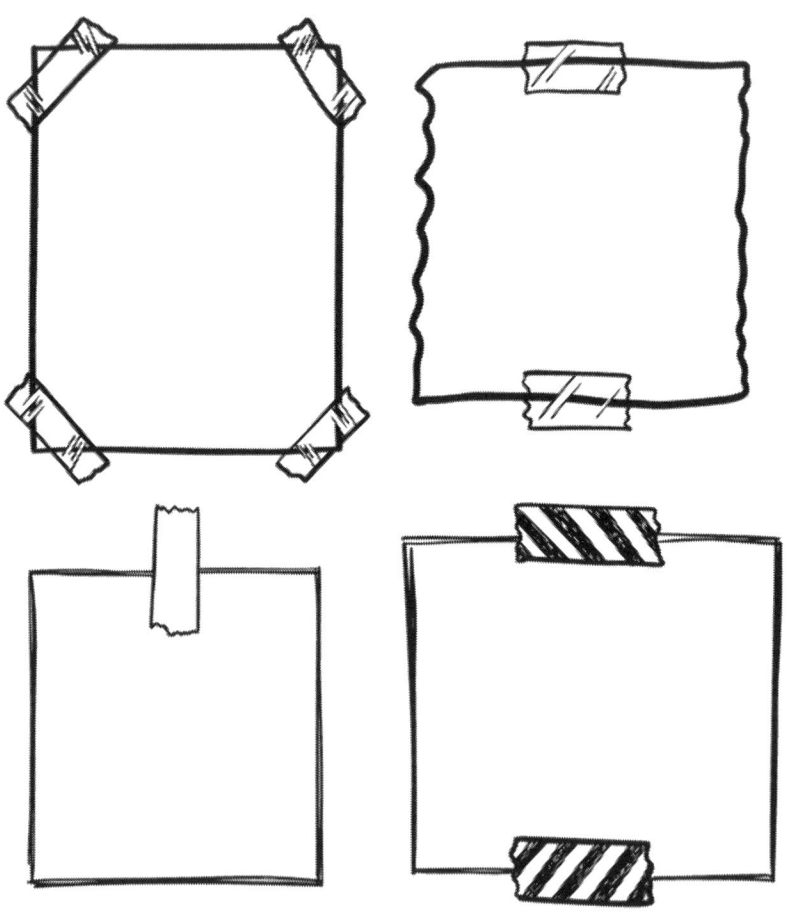

Study these Characters for Inspiration

Use Your own Characters in this Comic Strip

WHERE IN THE WORLD?

I am looking
for my shoe
I lost it yesterday.
Where in the world
is my shoe?
I want to go
outside and play.

COLOR ME!

WHERE IN THE WORLD?

I am _____
for my _____
I lost it _____.
where in the _____
Is my _____?
I _____ to go
_____ and play.

DRAW THE MISSING PARTS:

CREATE A COMIC
WITH THESE SPELLING WORDS:

lost

world

outside

shoe

yesterday

where

want

WHERE IN THE WORLD?

I am looking
for my shoe
I lost it yesterday.
Where in the world
is my shoe?
I want to go
outside and play.

COPY THE POEM HERE:

CREATIVE COMICS
DESIGN YOUR OWN CHARACTERS HERE

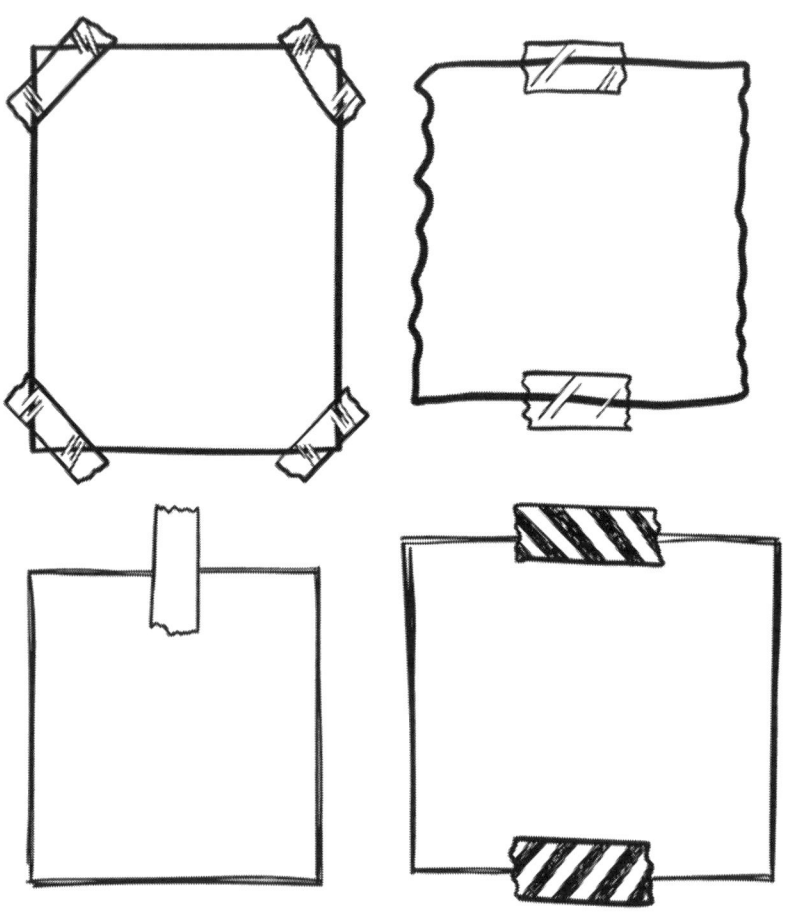

Study these Characters for Inspiration

Use Your own Characters in this Comic Strip

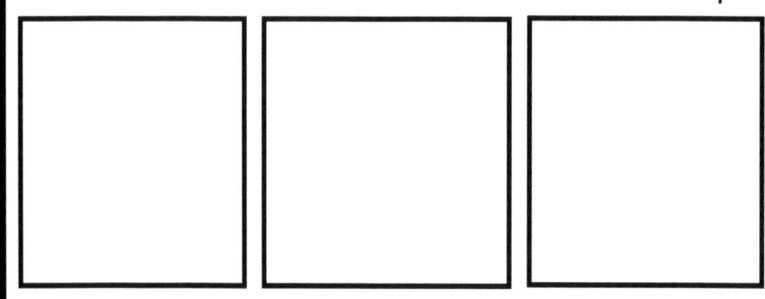

CAMPING TIME

We are going camping
in the woods.
We will cook
over the fires.
We are going hiking
In the woods.
We will bring our
snacks and wires.

COLOR ME!

CAMPING TIME

WE ARE GOING CAMPING
IN THE WOODS.
WE WILL COOK
OVER THE FIRES.
WE ARE GOING HIKING
IN THE WOODS.
WE WILL BRING OUR
SNACKS AND WIRES.

Use ten different colors to color all the words in this poem.

DRAW THE MISSING PARTS:

CREATE A COMIC
WITH THESE SPELLING WORDS:

 camping

 woods

cook

 fires

hiking

 snacks

 going

CAMPING TIME

We are going camping
in the woods.
We will cook
over the fires.
We are going hiking
in the woods.
We will bring our
snacks and wires.

COPY THE POEM HERE:

SPELLING TIME

Choose a letter:

Look in this book for 5 words that contain this letter.

1. _____
2. _____
3. _____
4. _____
5. _____

WRITE THESE FIVE WORDS IN CURSIVE

CREATIVE COMICS
DESIGN YOUR OWN CHARACTERS HERE

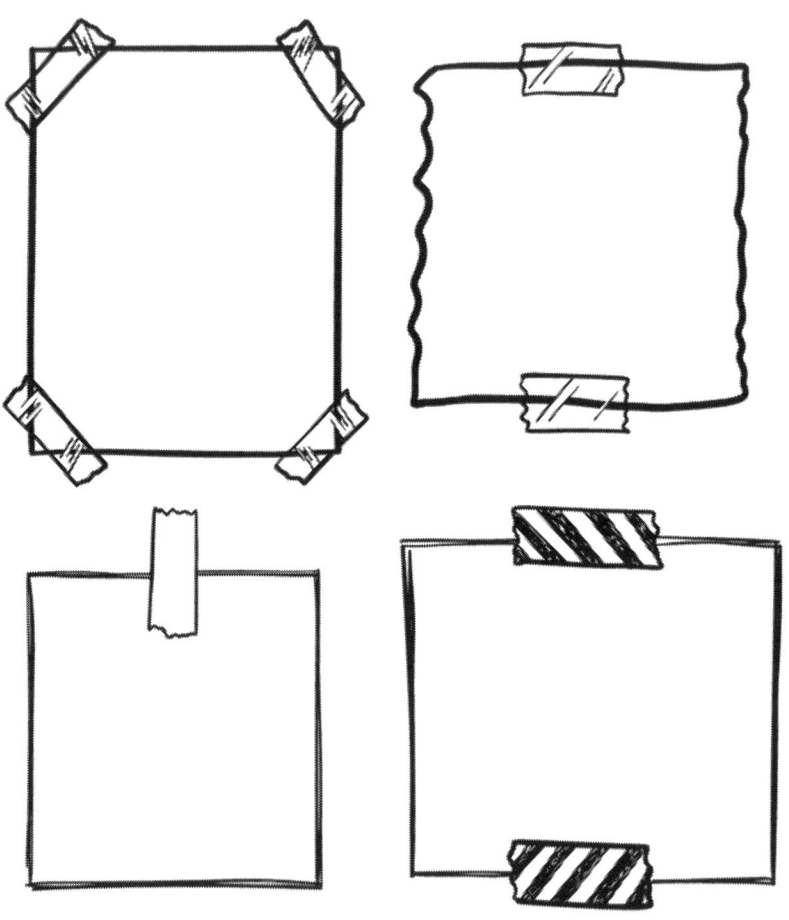

Study these Characters for Inspiration

Use Your own Characters in this Comic Strip

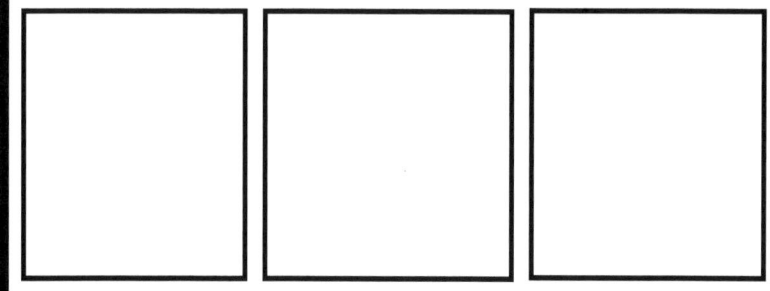

ALL MY PETS

I love my cat.
I love my dogs.
I love my birds.
I love my frogs.
I love my chicken
And my pig.
So many pets
for just one kid!

COLOR ME!

ALL MY PETS

I _____ my cat.
I love my _____.
I love my _____.
I love my _____.
I love my _____
and my pig.
So _____ pets
For _____ one kid!

DRAW THE MISSING PARTS:

CREATE A COMIC
WITH THESE SPELLING WORDS:

 love

 cat

dog

 birds

frogs

 chicken

pig

 kid

many

ALL MY PETS

I love my cat.
I love my dogs.
I love my birds.
I love my frogs.
I love my chicken
And my pig.
So many pets
For just one kid!

COPY THE POEM HERE:

DRAW A PICTURE

WRITE A POEM ABOUT YOUR PICTURE:

THINKING TIME

Every time I stop
to think,
A light shines
in my mind.
And when I stop
to dream a while,
My face becomes
a happy smile.

COLOR ME!

THINKING TIME

EVERY TIME I STOP
TO THINK,
A LIGHT SHINES
IN MY MIND.
AND WHEN I STOP
TO DREAM A WHILE,
MY FACE BECOMES
A HAPPY SMILE.

Use twelve different colors to color all the words in this poem.

DRAW THE MISSING PARTS:

CREATE A COMIC
WITH THESE SPELLING WORDS:

every

think

light

shines

mind

dream

while

smile

face

THINKING TIME

Every time I stop
to think,
A light shines
in my mind.
And when I stop
to dream a while,
My face becomes
a happy smile.

COPY THE POEM HERE:

SPELLING TIME

Choose a letter:

_____

Look in this book for 5 words that contain this letter.

1. _____
2. _____
3. _____
4. _____
5. _____

WRITE THESE FIVE WORDS IN CURSIVE

CREATIVE COMICS
DESIGN YOUR OWN CHARACTERS HERE

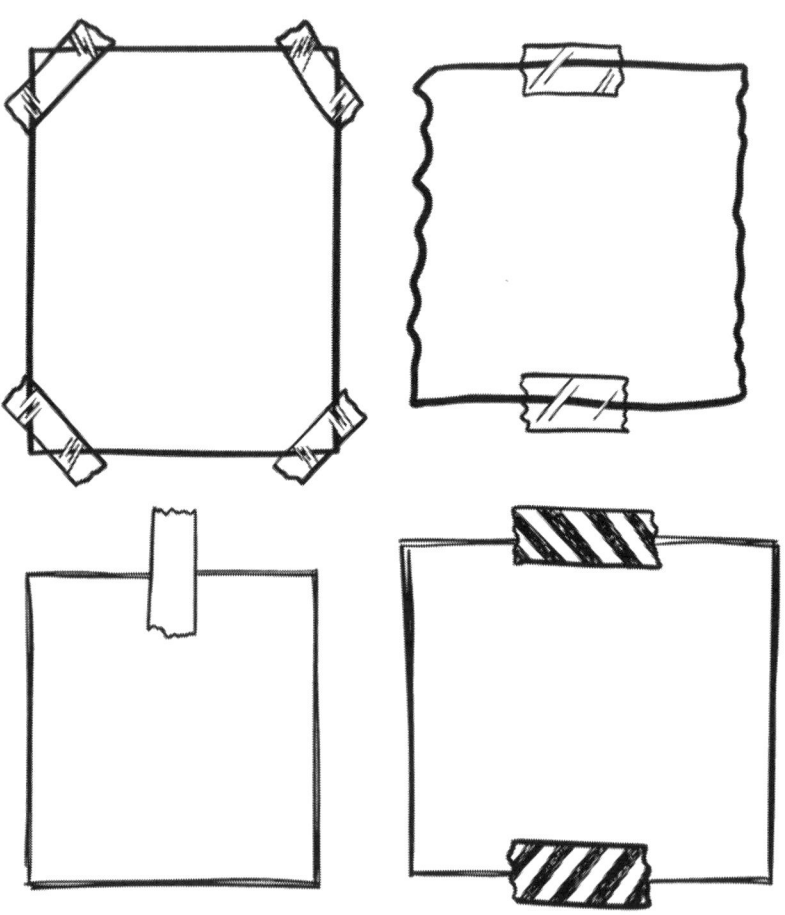

Study these Characters for Inspiration

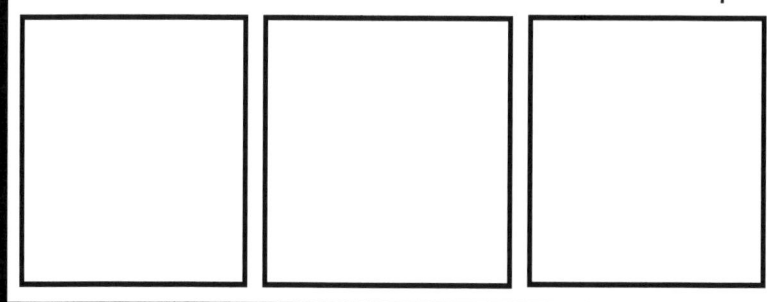

Use Your own Characters in this Comic Strip

THE AMAZING PENCIL

A pencil is
a simple thing,
but it has the
greatest powers.
It can create
stories and art,
when I use it
for three hours.

COLOR ME!

THE AMAZING PENCIL

A _____ is
a _____ thing,
but it has the
_____ powers.
It can _____
_____ and art,
when I use it
for _____ hours.

DRAW THE MISSING PARTS:

CREATE A COMIC
WITH THESE SPELLING WORDS:

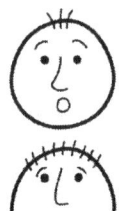

pencil

simple

greatest

powers

create

stories

art

use

hours

THE AMAZING PENCIL

A pencil is a simple thing, but it has the greatest powers. It can create stories and art, when I use it for three hours.

COPY THE POEM HERE:

dance	dream	every
dog	eagle	explored
dolphin	earth	face
doors	eat	favorite
down	eating	fires

TRY WRITING YOUR SPELLING WORDS WITH A COMIC STYLE FONT!

CREATIVE COMICS
DESIGN YOUR OWN CHARACTERS HERE

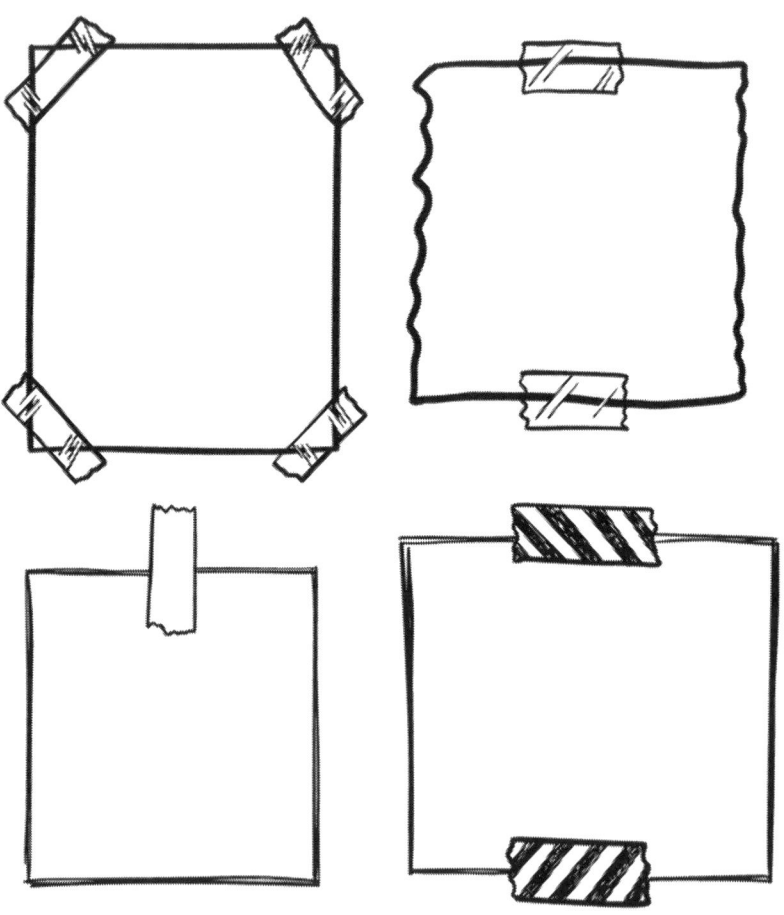

Study these Characters for Inspiration

Use Your own Characters in this Comic Strip

THE CANOE

What would you do,
if you had a canoe?
Where would you go
if you could row?
Would you float
in a little boat?
What would you do,
if you had a canoe?

COLOR ME!

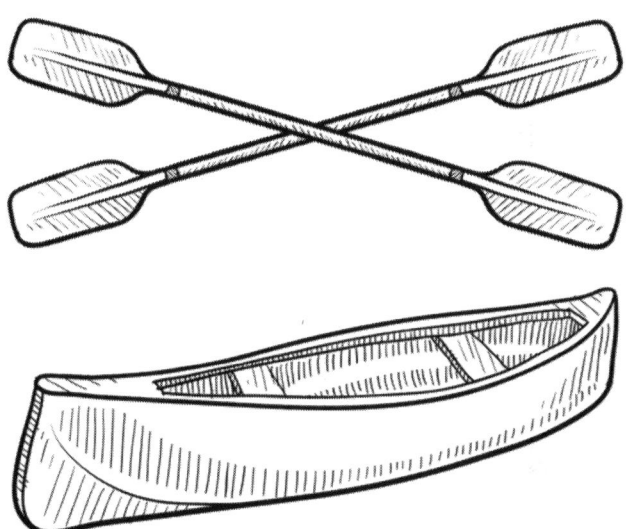

THE CANOE

WHAT WOULD YOU DO,
IF YOU HAD A CANOE?
WHERE WOULD YOU GO
IF YOU COULD ROW?
WOULD YOU FLOAT
IN A LITTLE BOAT?
WHAT WOULD YOU DO,
IF YOU HAD A CANOE?

Use four different colors to color all the words in this poem.

DRAW THE MISSING PARTS:

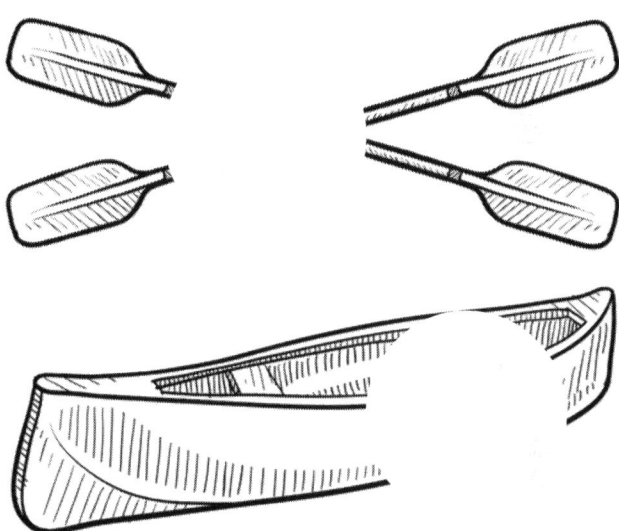

CREATE A COMIC
WITH THESE SPELLING WORDS:

what

would

had

where

could

float

boat

canoe

row

THE CANOE

What would you do,

if you had a canoe?

Where would you go

if you could row?

Would you float

in a little boat?

What would you do,

if you had a canoe?

COPY THE POEM HERE:

DRAW A PICTURE

WRITE A POEM ABOUT YOUR PICTURE:

CUPCAKES

My little sister

likes to bake.

When she bakes

she makes some cakes.

Little cakes,

The perfect size.

I could eat

just four or five.

COLOR ME!

CUPCAKES

My little _____
likes to _____.
When she bakes
she _____ some cakes.
_____ cakes,
The _____ size.
I _____ eat
just _____ or five.

DRAW THE MISSING PARTS:

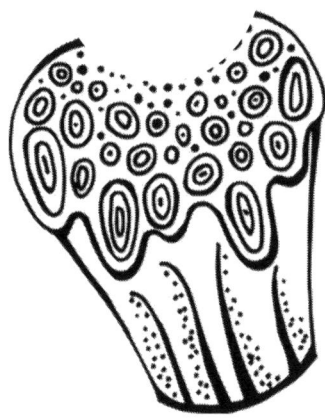

CREATE A COMIC
WITH THESE SPELLING WORDS:

 cupcakes

sister

 bakes

makes

 cakes

perfect

 size

eat

 just

CUPCAKES

My little sister
likes to bake.
When she bakes
she makes some cakes.
Little cakes,
the perfect size.
I could eat
just four or five.

COPY THE POEM HERE:

SPELLING TIME

Choose a letter:

Look in this book for 5 words that contain this letter.

1._____

2._____

3._____

4._____

5._____

WRITE THESE FIVE WORDS IN CURSIVE

A B C D E F G
H I J K L M
N O P Q R S T
U V W X Y Z

a b c d e f g h
i j k l m n o p
q r s t u v w x
y z 1 2 3 4 5 6 7 8 9 0

CREATIVE COMICS
DESIGN YOUR OWN CHARACTERS HERE

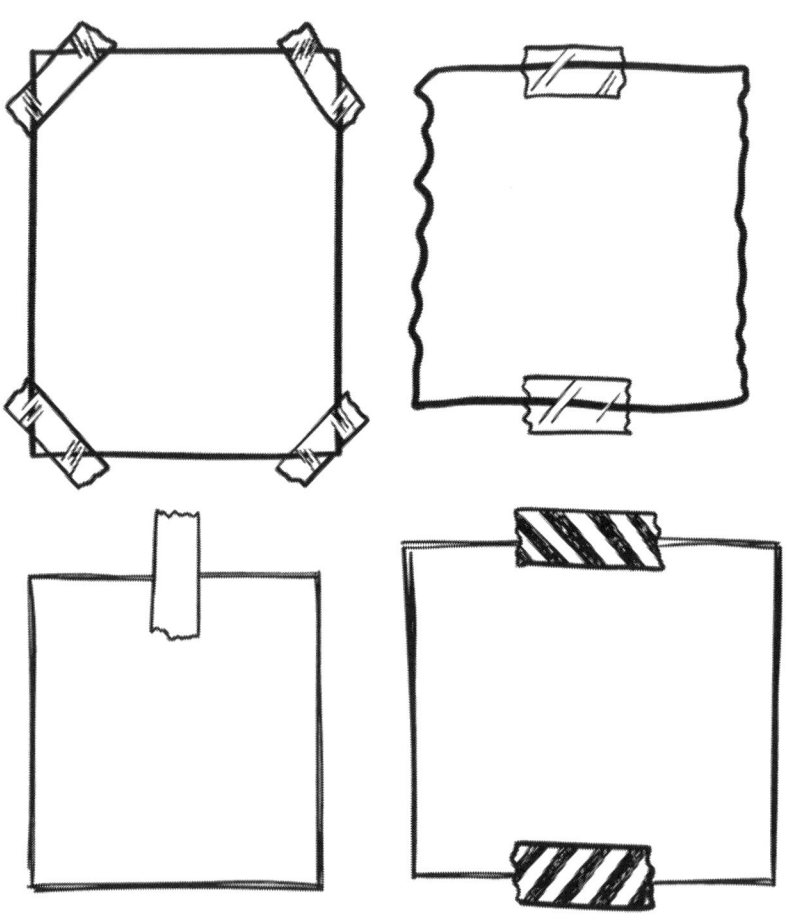

Study these Characters for Inspiration

Use Your own Characters in this Comic Strip

LOST APPLE

I was looking
for my hat.
And eating apples too.
I found my hat,
but lost my apple!
Oh no!
What shall I do?

COLOR ME!

LOST APPLE

I was _____
For my hat.
And _____ apples too.
I _____ my hat,
but lost my _____!
Oh no!
What _____ I do?

DRAW THE MISSING PARTS:

CREATE A COMIC
WITH THESE SPELLING WORDS:

 looking

 eating

apples

 found

lost

 perfect

shall

 what

was

LOST APPLE

I was looking
for my hat.
And eating apples too.
I found my hat,
but lost my apple!
Oh no!
What shall I do?

COPY THE POEM HERE:

CREATIVE COMICS
DESIGN YOUR OWN CHARACTERS HERE

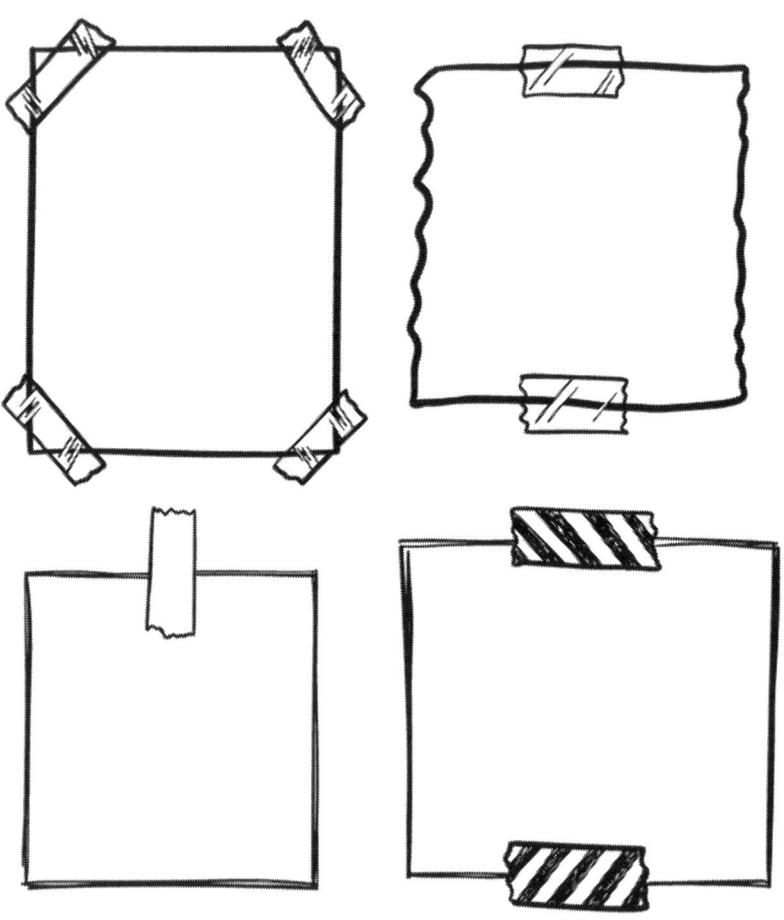

Study these Characters for Inspiration

Use Your own Characters in this Comic Strip

MY TREE

The year that I was born,
my mom planted a tree.
I love to watch it grow,
because it is
as old as me.
When I was little,
it was small.
now I am big,
and it is tall.

MY TREE

THE YEAR THAT I WAS BORN,
MY MOM PLANTED A TREE.
I LOVE TO WATCH IT GROW,
BECAUSE IT IS
AS OLD AS ME.
WHEN I WAS LITTLE,
IT WAS SMALL.
NOW I AM BIG,
AND IT IS TALL.

DRAW THE MISSING PARTS:

CREATE A COMIC
WITH THESE SPELLING WORDS:

year

born

planted

tree

watch

because

small

tall

grow

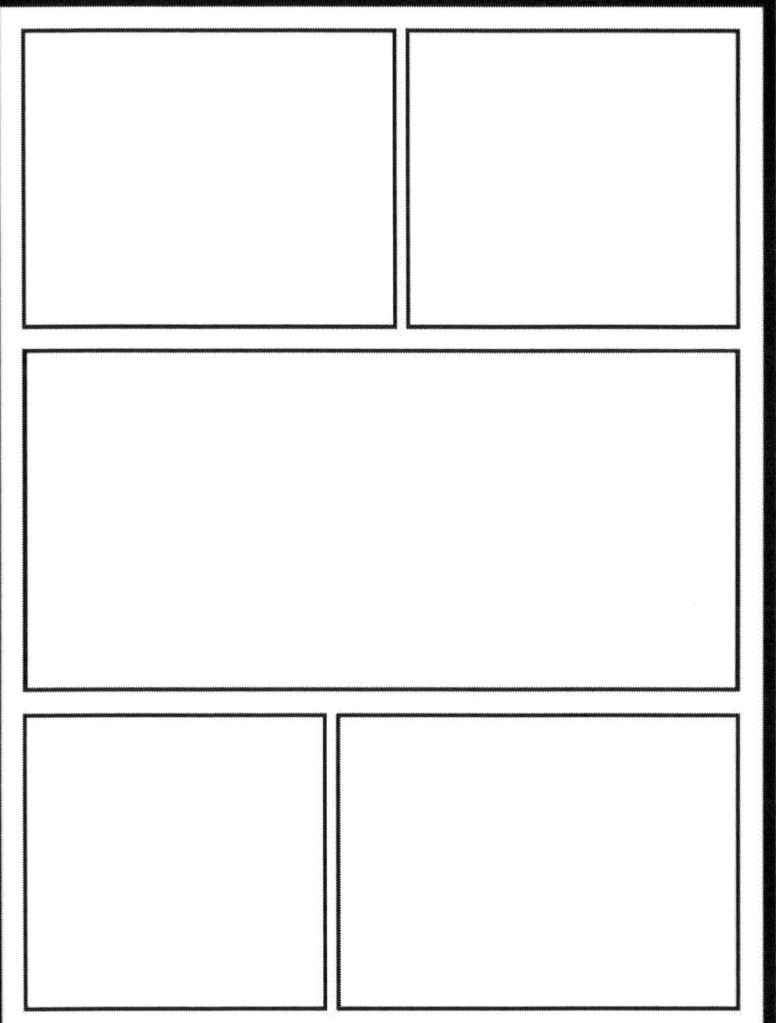

MY TREE

The year that I was born,

my mom planted a tree.

I love to watch it grow,

because it is

as old as me.

When I was little,

it was small.

Now I am big,

and it is tall.

COPY THE POEM HERE:

CREATIVE COMICS
DESIGN YOUR OWN CHARACTERS HERE

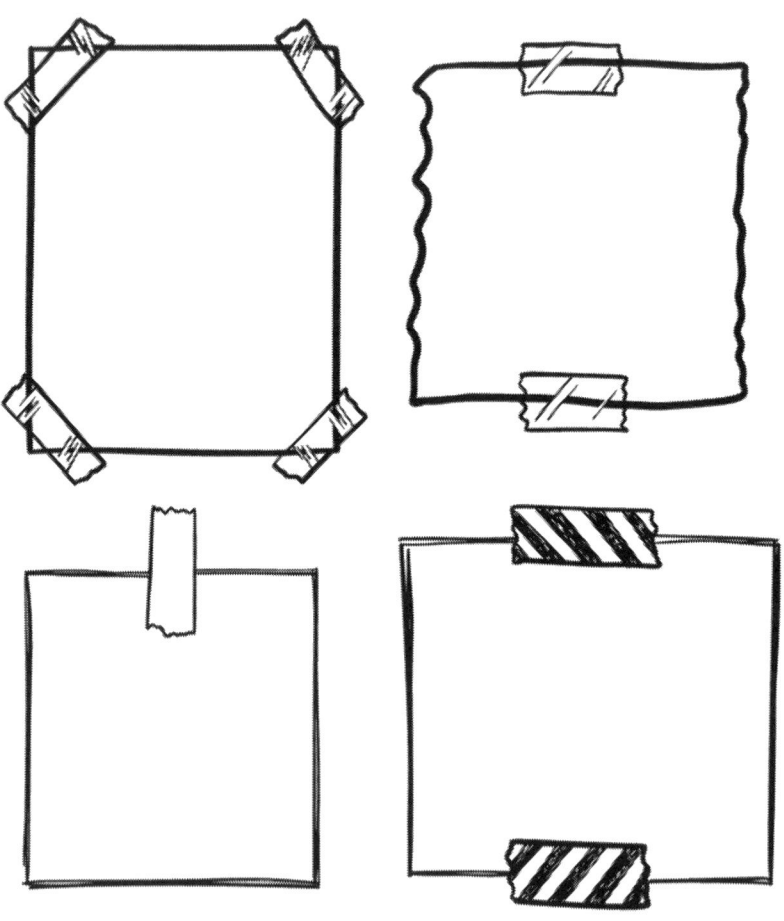

Study these Characters for Inspiration

Use Your own Characters in this Comic Strip

dance	dream	every
dog	eagle	explored
dolphin	earth	face
doors	eat	favorite
down	eating	fires

TRY WRITING YOUR SPELLING WORDS WITH A COMIC STYLE FONT!

SEASHELLS

In the summer
I will be
running up and
down the beach!
I will play
hide and seek,
And search for seashells
by the sea!

COLOR ME!

SEASHELLS

In the _____
I will be
_____ up and
down the _____!
I ____ play
____ and seek,
and _____ for
seashells
by the ___!

DRAW THE MISSING PARTS:

CREATE A COMIC
WITH THESE SPELLING WORDS:

 summer

 running

down

 beach

hide

 seek

search

 seashells

sea

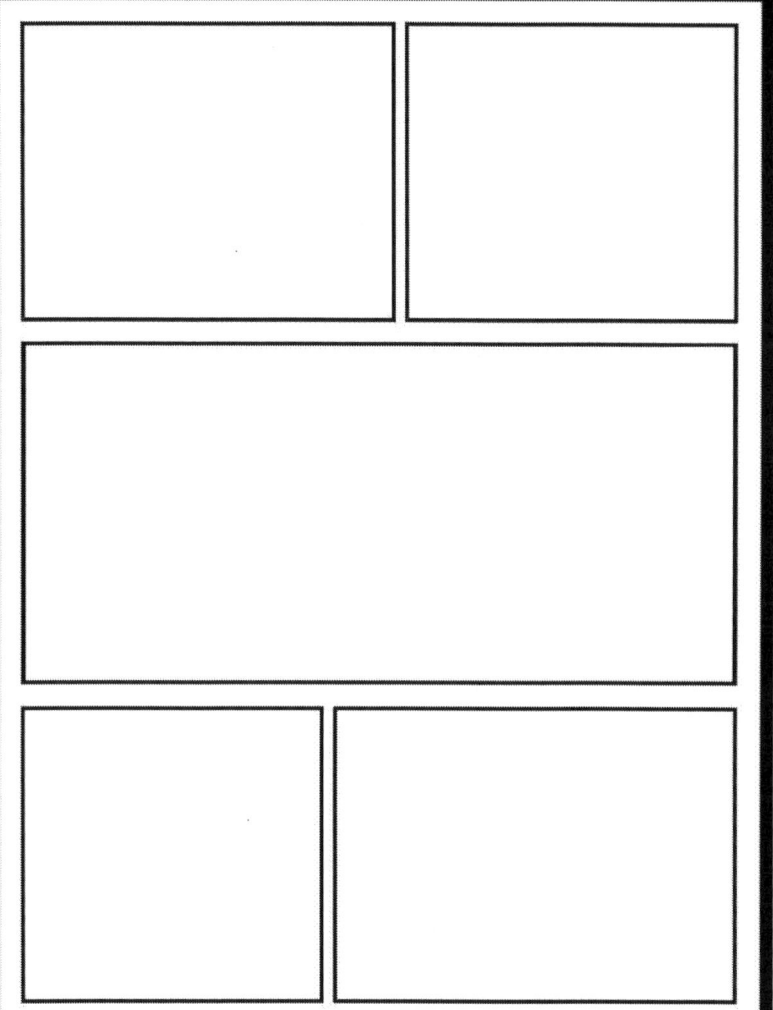

SEASHELLS

In the summer
I will be
running up and
down the beach!
I will play
hide and seek,
and search for seashells
by the sea!

COPY THE POEM HERE:

SPELLING TIME

Choose a letter:

Look in this book for 5 words that contain this letter.

1. _____

2. _____

3. _____

4. _____

5. _____

WRITE THESE FIVE WORDS IN CURSIVE

CREATIVE COMICS
DESIGN YOUR OWN CHARACTERS HERE

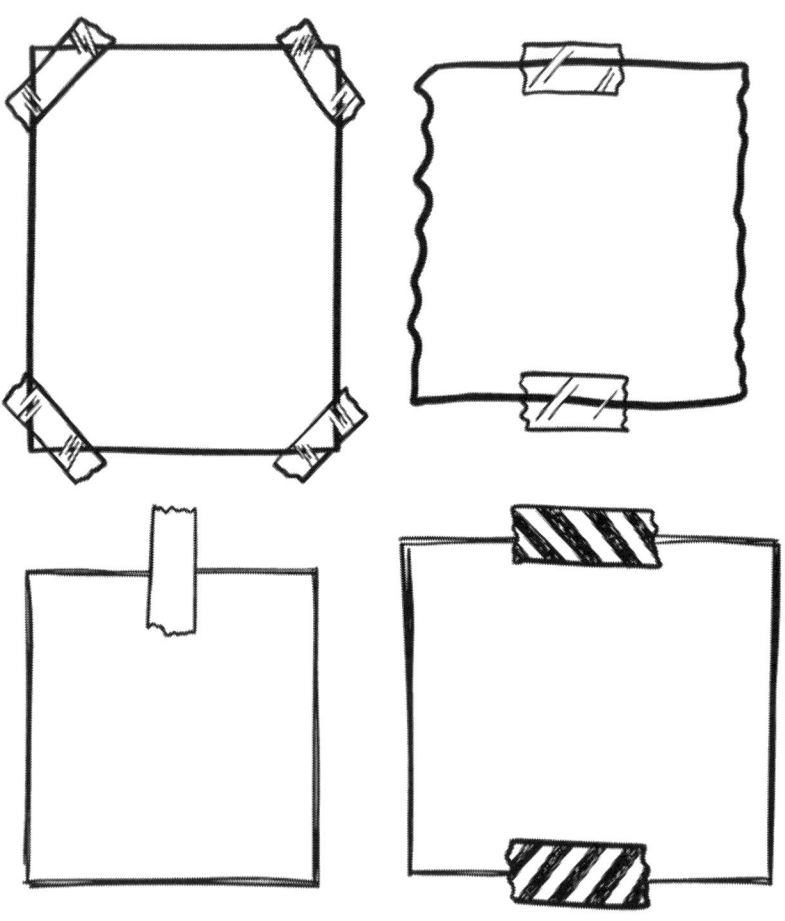

Study these Characters for Inspiration

Use Your own Characters in this Comic Strip

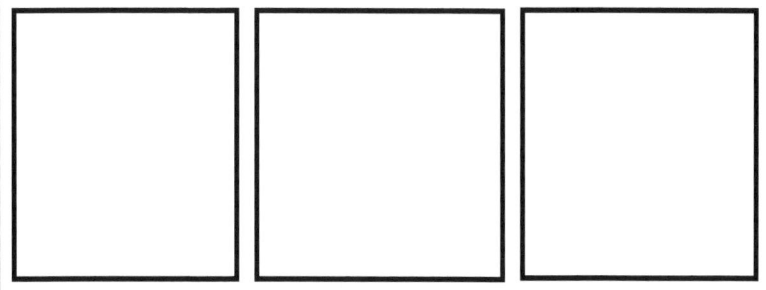

PANCAKES

On Saturday
I wake up late
and smell some
yummy food!
No time to play,
let's start the day!
I'm in a
pancake mood!

PANCAKES

ON SATURDAY
I WAKE UP LATE
AND SMELL SOME
YUMMY FOOD!
NO TIME TO PLAY,
LET'S START THE DAY!
I'M IN A
PANCAKE MOOD!

Use twenty different colors to color all the words in this poem.

DRAW THE MISSING PARTS:

CREATE A COMIC
WITH THESE SPELLING WORDS:

 Saturday

wake

 late

smell

 some

yummy

 start

pancake

 mood

food

PANCAKES

On Saturday
I wake up late
and smell some
yummy food!
No time to play,
let's start the day!
I'm in a
pancake mood!

COPY THE POEM HERE:

CREATIVE COMICS
DESIGN YOUR OWN CHARACTERS HERE

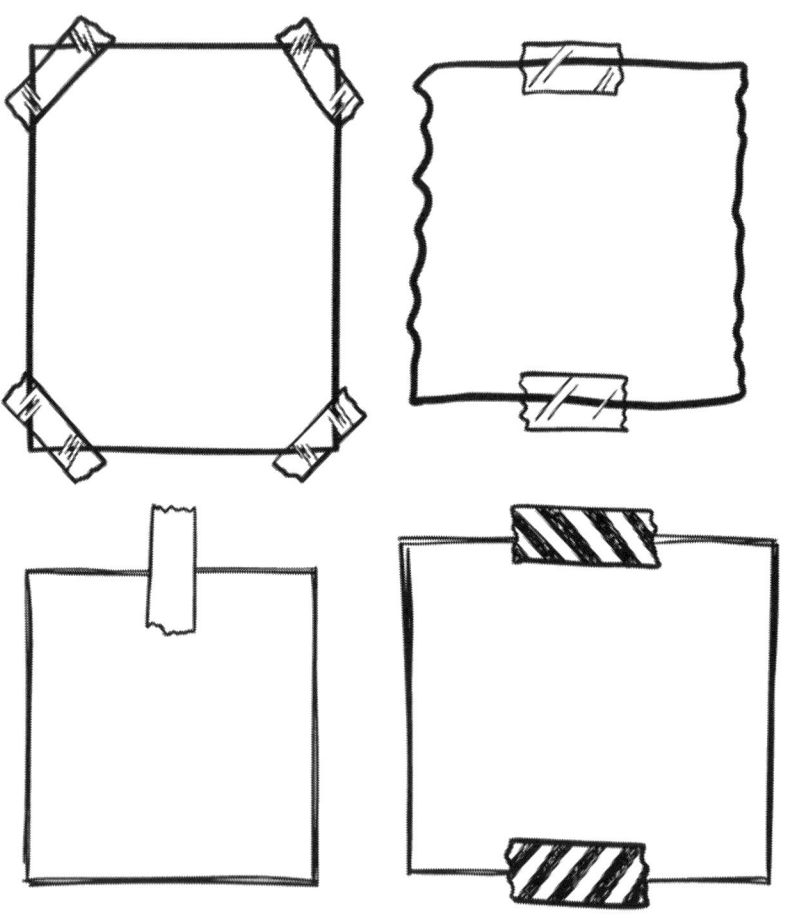

Study these Characters for Inspiration

Use Your own Characters in this Comic Strip

THE CASTLE

Last night I had a dream
I think you had one too.
I can't remember much,
but just one thing is true.
Last night I met a king
and a little princess too.
I explored a castle,
and tasted royal food!

THE CASTLE

Last _____ I had a _____
I _____ you had one too.
I can't _____ much,
but just one _____ is true.
Last _____ I met a king
and a little _____ too.
I _____ a castle,
and _____ royal food!

DRAW THE MISSING PARTS:

CREATE A COMIC
WITH THESE SPELLING WORDS:

 night

remember

 much

castle

 true

king

 princess

explored

 tasted

royal

THE CASTLE

Last night I had a dream

I think you had one too.

I can't remember much,

but just one thing is true.

Last night I met a king

and a little princess too.

I explored a castle,

and tasted royal food!

COPY THE POEM HERE:

DRAW A PICTURE

WRITE A POEM ABOUT YOUR PICTURE:

ANIMALS

I love to swim,

I am a dolphin.

I love to sing,

I am a canary.

I love to fly,

I am an eagle.

I love to play,

I am a puppy.

COLOR ME!

ANIMALS

I LOVE TO SWIM,
I AM A DOLPHIN.
I LOVE TO SING,
I AM A CANARY.
I LOVE TO FLY,
I AM A EAGLE.
I LOVE TO PLAY,
I AM A PUPPY.

Use nine different colors to color all the words in this poem.

DRAW THE MISSING PARTS:

CREATE A COMIC
WITH THESE SPELLING WORDS:

dolphin

swim

canary

sing

eagle

fly

puppy

play

animals

ANIMALS

I love to swim,

I am a dolphin.

I love to sing,

I am a canary.

I love to fly,

I am an eagle.

I love to play,

I am a puppy.

COPY THE POEM HERE:

SPELLING TIME

Choose a letter:

Look in this book for 5 words that contain this letter.

1. _____

2. _____

3. _____

4. _____

5. _____

WRITE THESE FIVE WORDS IN CURSIVE

CREATIVE COMICS
DESIGN YOUR OWN CHARACTERS HERE

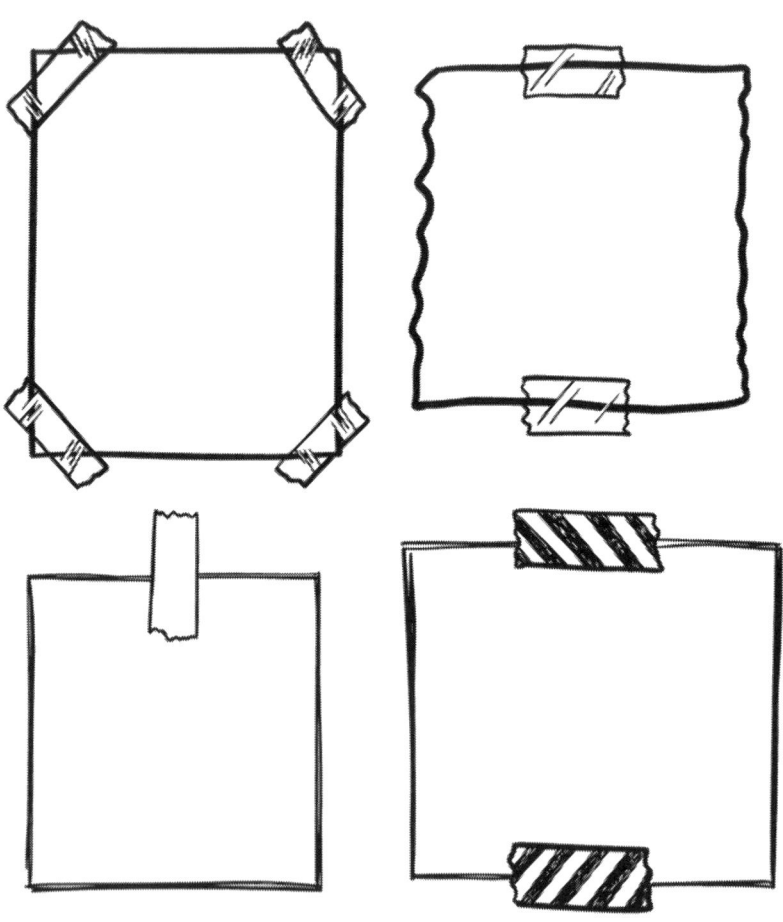

Study these Characters for Inspiration

Use Your own Characters in this Comic Strip

PUPPY LOVE

My best friend
is a puppy.
My puppy
is so cute.
He loves to play.
He loves to jump.
He loves to
chew on boots!

COLOR ME!

PUPPY LOVE

My best _____
is a puppy.
My _____
is so cute.
He _____ to play.
He loves to jump.
He loves to
____ on boots!

DRAW THE MISSING PARTS:

CREATE A COMIC
WITH THESE SPELLING WORDS:

 best

friend

 loves

puppy

 cute

 loves

jump

 chew

PUPPY LOVE

My best friend
is a puppy.
My puppy
is so cute.
He loves to play.
He loves to jump
He loves to
chew on boots!

COPY THE POEM HERE:

fit	found	going
float	friend	greatest
fluffy	friends	grow
fly	frogs	had
food	from	hallway

TRY WRITING YOUR SPELLING WORDS WITH A COMIC STYLE FONT!

CREATIVE COMICS
DESIGN YOUR OWN CHARACTERS HERE

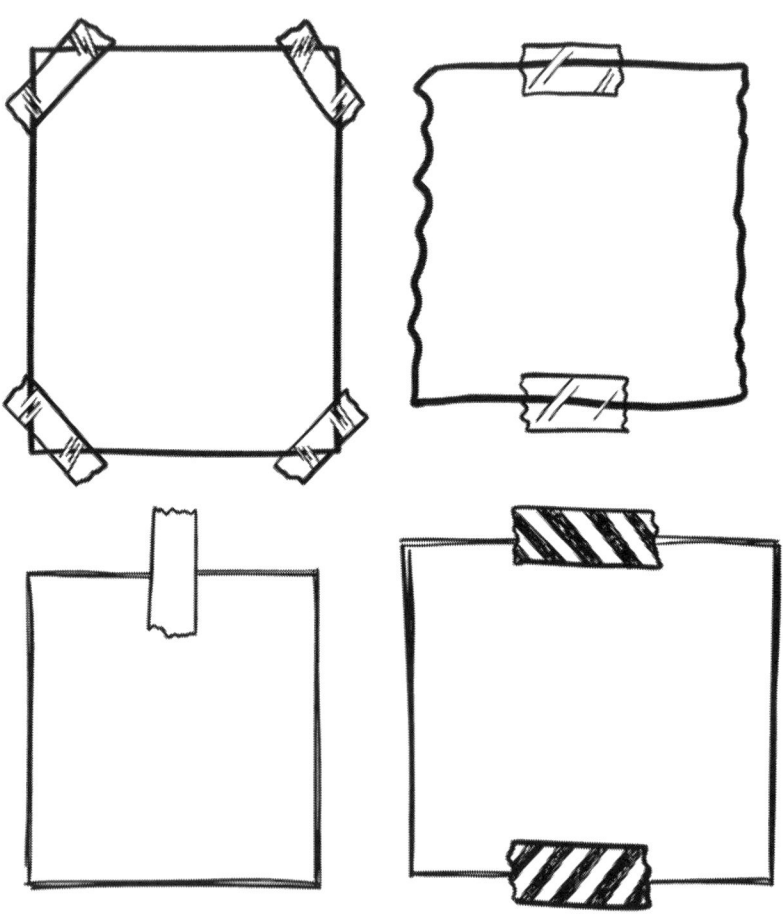

Study these Characters for Inspiration

Use Your own Characters in this Comic Strip

SWEET THINGS

The yummy treats
I love to eat
are ice-cream,
pies and cake!
I know that sweets
Can rot my teeth.
If I eat them
every day!

COLOR ME!

SWEET THINGS

THE YUMMY TREATS
I LOVE TO EAT
ARE ICE-CREAM,
PIES AND CAKE!
I KNOW THAT SWEETS
CAN ROT MY TEETH.
IF I EAT THEM
EVERY DAY!

Use eight different colors to color all the words in this poem.

DRAW THE MISSING PARTS:

CREATE A COMIC
WITH THESE SPELLING WORDS:

- treats
- Ice-cream
- pies
- cake
- know
- sweets
- teeth
- them
- every

SWEET THINGS

The yummy treats
I love to eat
are ice-cream,
pies and cake!
I know that sweets
Can rot my teeth.
If I eat them
every day!

COPY THE POEM HERE:

CREATIVE COMICS
DESIGN YOUR OWN CHARACTERS HERE

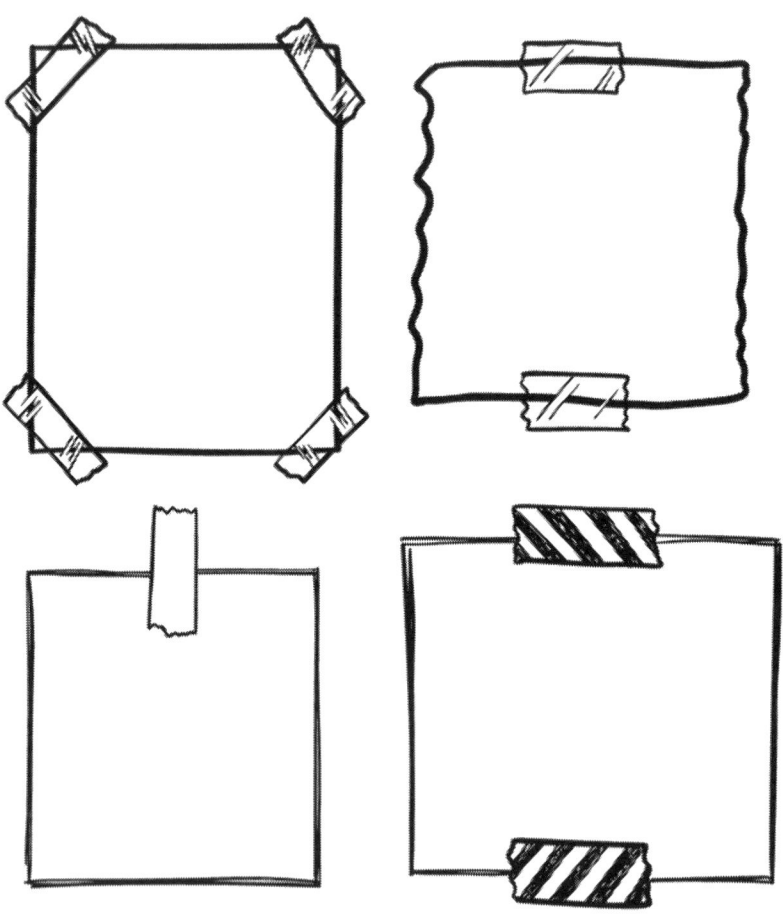

Study these Characters for Inspiration

Use Your own Characters in this Comic Strip

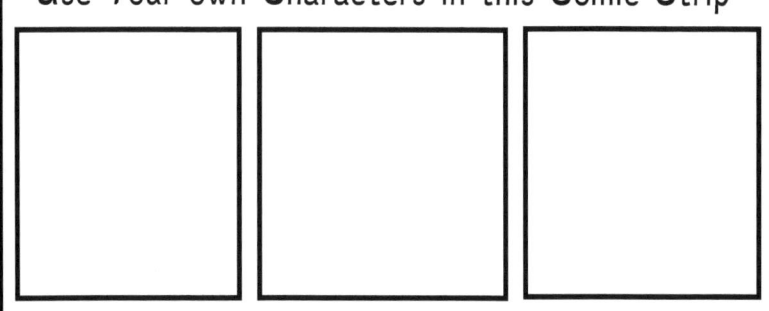

TINY-TOOT

When my puppy
was a baby
I named him
Tiny-Toot!
He was fluffy,
white and shaggy.
He could fit
inside my boot!

COLOR ME!

TINY-TOOT

When my _____
was a ____
I _____ him
Tiny-Toot!
He was _____,
_____ and shaggy.
He _____ fit
inside __ boot!

DRAW THE MISSING PARTS:

CREATE A COMIC
WITH THESE SPELLING WORDS:

 baby

named

 fluffy

white

 shaggy

fit

 could

inside

 tiny

TINY-TOOT

When my puppy
was a baby
I named him
Tiny-Toot!
He was fluffy,
white and shaggy.
He could fit
inside my boot!

COPY THE POEM HERE:

SPELLING TIME

Choose a letter:

Look in this book for 5 words that contain this letter.

1._____

2._____

3._____

4._____

5._____

WRITE THESE FIVE WORDS IN CURSIVE

CREATIVE COMICS
DESIGN YOUR OWN CHARACTERS HERE

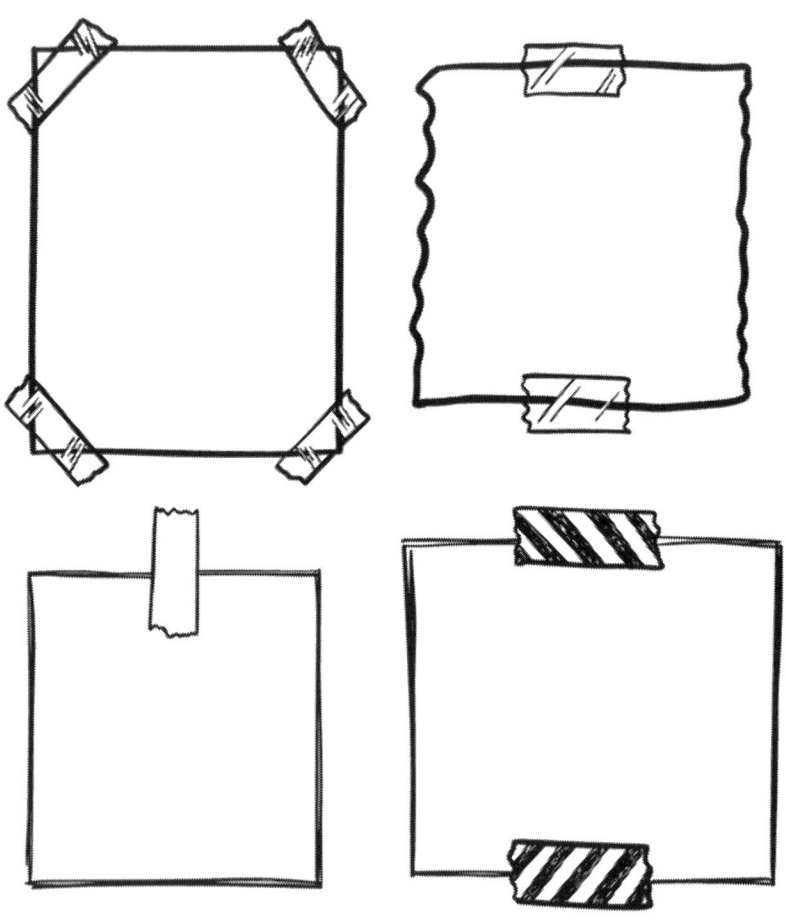

Study these Characters for Inspiration

Use Your own Characters in this Comic Strip

PILLOW TIME

I searched my house
for pillows.
I looked in
every room.
I stacked them
In the hallway.
They almost
reached the moon.

COLOR ME!

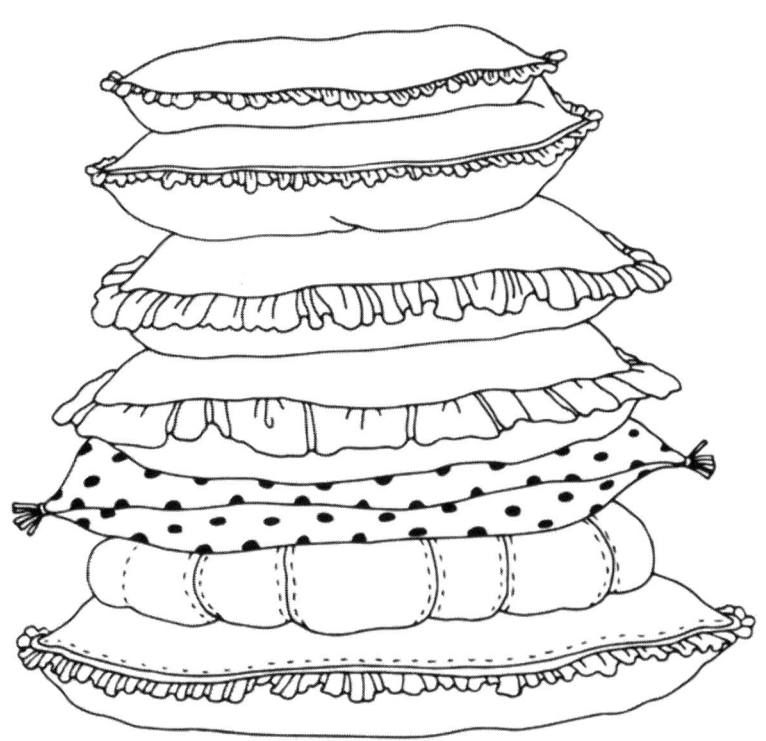

PILLOW TIME

I SEARCHED MY HOUSE
FOR PILLOWS.
I LOOKED IN
EVERY ROOM.
I STACKED THEM
IN THE HALLWAY.
THEY ALMOST
REACHED THE MOON.

Use four different colors to color all the words in this poem.

DRAW THE MISSING PARTS:

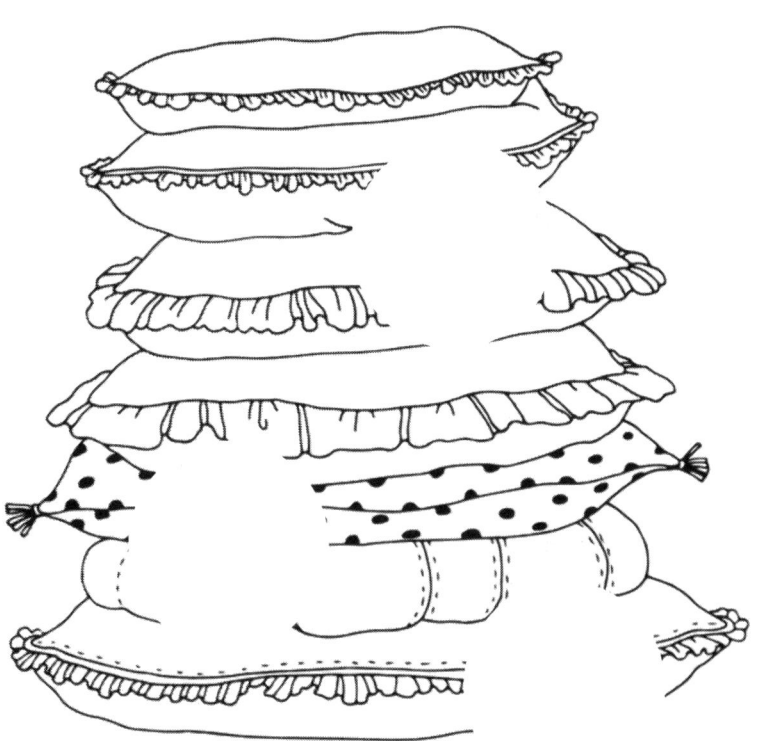

CREATE A COMIC
WITH THESE SPELLING WORDS:

searched

house

pillows

looked

stacked

hallway

almost

reached

moon

PILLOW TIME

I searched my house
for pillows
I looked in
every room.
I stacked them
In the hallway.
They almost
reached the moon.

COPY THE POEM HERE:

CREATIVE COMICS
DESIGN YOUR OWN CHARACTERS HERE

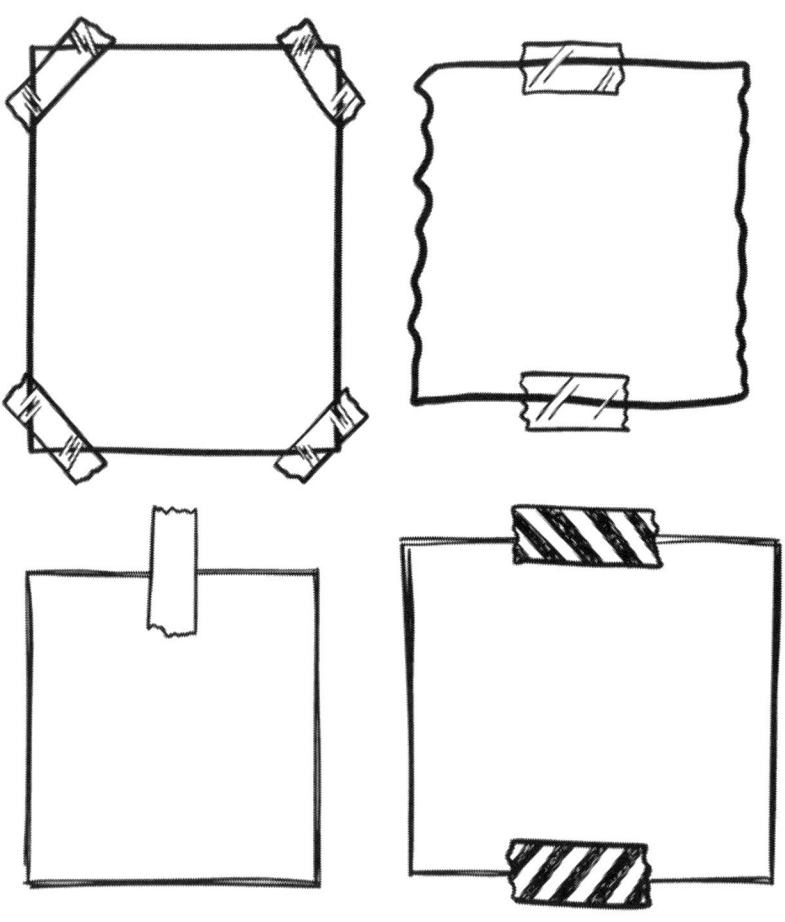

Study these Characters for Inspiration

Use Your own Characters in this Comic Strip

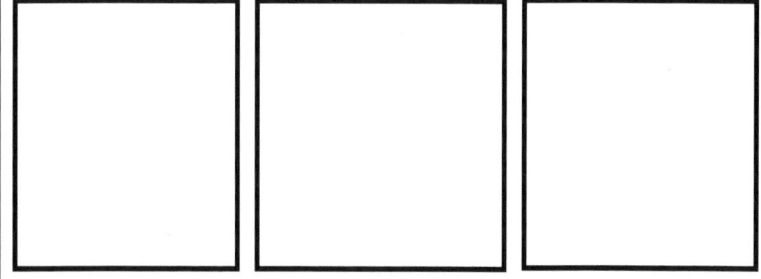

OWL FRIENDS

My owl friends
live in the tree.
They sing and hunt
at night.
I watch them
from my window
when I stay up
late at night.

COLOR ME!

OWL FRIENDS

My ___ friends
live in the _____.
They _____ and hunt
at night.
I watch them
From my _____
when I stay up
late at _____.

DRAW THE MISSING PARTS:

CREATE A COMIC
WITH THESE SPELLING WORDS:

owl

friends

live

hunt

watch

stay

from

night

late

they

OWL FRIENDS

My owl friends
live in the tree.
They sing and hunt
At night.
I watch them
from my window
when I stay up
late at night.

COPY THE POEM HERE:

DRAW A PICTURE

WRITE A POEM ABOUT YOUR PICTURE:

SPELLING TIME

Choose a letter:

_____

Look in this book for 5 words that contain this letter.

1. _____

2. _____

3. _____

4. _____

5. _____

WRITE THESE FIVE WORDS IN CURSIVE

𝒶 𝐵 𝒞 𝒟 𝐸 𝐹 𝒢
𝐻 𝐼 𝒥 𝒦 𝐿 𝑀
𝑛 𝒪 𝒫 𝒬 𝑅 𝒮 𝒯
𝒰 𝒱 𝒲 𝒳 𝒴 𝒵

𝒶 𝒷 𝒸 𝒹 𝑒 𝒻 𝑔 𝒽
𝒾 𝒿 𝓀 𝓁 𝓂 𝓃 𝑜 𝓅
𝓆 𝓇 𝓈 𝓉 𝓊 𝓋 𝓌 𝓍
𝓎 𝓏 1 2 3 4 5 6 7 8 9 0

HAPPY HOUSE

I love my
happy little house.
My cats all love it too.
I love the
doors and windows
And the rooster on the roof.

COLOR ME!

HAPPY HOUSE

I love __
happy little _____.
My cats all love it ____.
I love ___
doors and _____
And the _____
on the _____.

DRAW THE MISSING PARTS:

CREATE A COMIC
WITH THESE SPELLING WORDS:

 love

happy

 little

house

 doors

windows

 rooster

roof

 my

HAPPY HOUSE

I love my
happy little house.
My cats all love it too.
I love the
doors and windows
And the rooster
on the roof.

COPY THE POEM HERE:

SPELLING TIME

Choose a letter:

_____

Look in this book for 5 words that contain this letter.

1._____

2._____

3._____

4._____

5._____

WRITE THESE FIVE WORDS IN CURSIVE

hiking	ice-cream	know
home	inside	late
hours	just	learn
house	kid	light
hunt	king	listen

TRY WRITING YOUR SPELLING WORDS WITH A COMIC STYLE FONT!

CREATIVE COMICS
DESIGN YOUR OWN CHARACTERS HERE

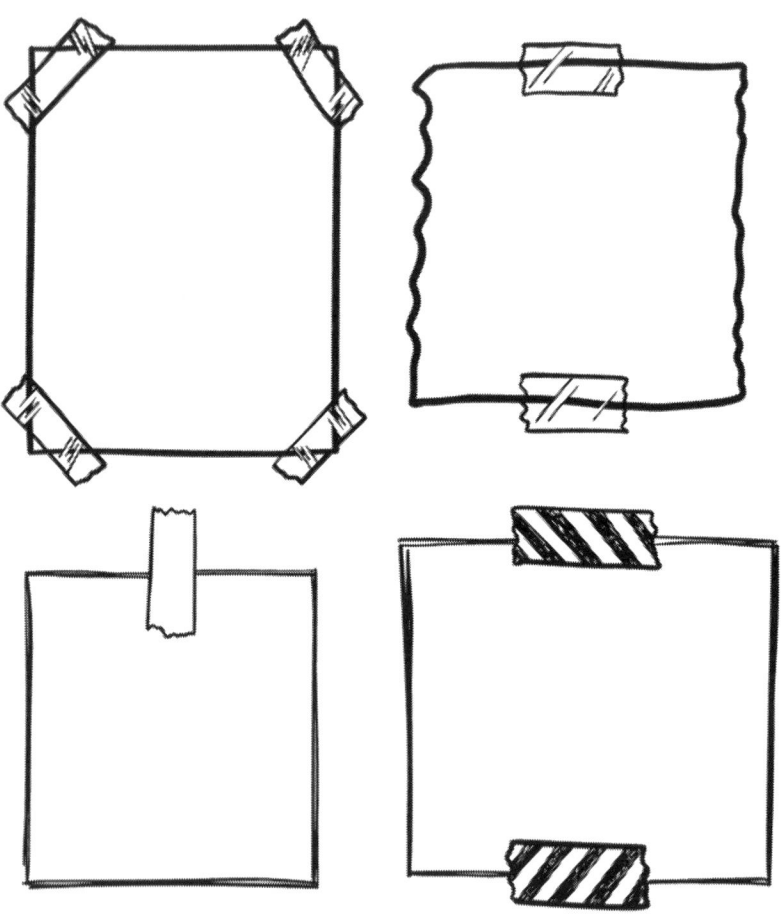

Study these Characters for Inspiration

Use Your own Characters in this Comic Strip

Made in the USA
Middletown, DE
13 February 2019